D0624787

bow-er-bird (bau'er burd), *n.* any of several birds of the family Ptilonorhynchidae, of Australia, New Guinea, and adjacent islands, the males of which build bower-like, decorated structures, arched over with twigs and grasses, often adorned with bright-colored objects such as feathers, bones, shells, glass, and plastic. These are not used as nests, but rather as places to attract the female.

Su-san L. Roth (su'zan ell roth), *n.* an illustrator and author of more than fifty books for children. She works exclusively in collage using bright-colored papers from all over the world as well as other objects such as feathers, fabrics, wires, pipe cleaners, string, glass, and plastic.

BIRDS OF A FEATHER

BIRDS OF A FEATHER

BOWERBIRDS AND ME

SUSAN L. ROTH

NEAL PORTER BOOKS
HOLIDAY HOUSE / NEW YORK

Neal Porter Books

Text and illustrations copyright © 2019 by Susan L. Roth

All Rights Reserved

HOLIDAY HOUSE is registered in the U.S. Patent and Trademark Office.

Printed and bound in October 2018 at Toppan Leefung, DongGuan City, China.

The art for this book was created with assorted papers, fabric, wires, threads, pipe cleaners,
beads, ribbons, and more, especially those that are bright blue.

Book design by Jennifer Browne

www.holidayhouse.com

First Edition

2 4 8 6 8 10 9 7 5 3 1

Library of Congress Cataloging-in-Publication Data

Names: Roth, Susan L., author.
Title: Birds of a feather : bowerbirds and me / Susan L. Roth.
Description: First edition. | New York : Holiday House, 2019. | "Neal Porter
Books." | Includes bibliographical references. | Audience: K to Grade 3
Identifiers: LCCN 2018028236 | ISBN 9780823442829 (hardcover)
Subjects: LCSH: Roth, Susan L.—Themes, motives—Juvenile literature. |
Collage—United States—Juvenile literature. |
Bowerbirds—Miscellanea—Juvenile literature.
Classification: LCC N6537.R6282 A35 2019 | DDC 709.2—dc23 LC record available at
https://lccn.loc.gov/2018028236

FOR JESSE, WITH LOVE, SL

The differences between a bowerbird and me are fewer than you might expect.

We are both
collectors
of unusual,
often unrelated
stuff

that we use
in unusual ways
to create different and unexpected compositions
in rather small, defined spaces.

Our serious purpose is to have the results be
as beautiful as we can make them:
mine, to tell
a story;

his, to attract
a mate.

We never make
any two of our
compositions
the same,

and even though our tools
are not identical,
they can easily be compared:
his beak operates like tweezers
and his feet are like my hands.
Even though they aren't
the same,
we expect them to do
the same tricks.

We each try hard
to give our delicate
compositions
some solidity.

Where do we get our ideas?
We get them
from the spaces we choose
for our compositions,
from our chosen materials,
and from the world around us.

We both like unusual objects
of manageable size.
We try to be original
in our sometimes ridiculous
arrangements
of things that most people
and most birds
would never in a million years
dream of putting together.

We love colors
that we try to use bravely,
and we both
are dependent
upon nature and
on manufactured junk
for our art supplies.

As with all artists,
we both seek praise;

and we both hope that our
finished works
are much greater
than the sum of their parts.

FACTS ABOUT BOWERBIRDS

1 BOWERBIRDS are birds that live on the east coast of Australia and the wilds of New Guinea.

2 Bowerbirds are named for the bowers that male bowerbirds build to attract their mates.

3 A bower is a recess, sheltered or covered with foliage—an arbor. It can also be a structure created by the male bowerbird, made of twigs and grasses. The floor is where the birds create their collages.

4 There are twenty different species of bowerbirds.

5 The bowers are NOT their nests. They are more like an artist's studio, where they work until their creations are complete. Then their bowers become places for display and mating.

6 Early references to these birds can be found in ancient Aboriginal legends. The bowerbird featured in my book is the SATIN BOWERBIRD (*Ptilonorhynchus violaceus*). This species lives primarily in New South Wales, Australia, but also in Queensland and Victoria. A second subspecies is found in the Atherton Tableland in north Queensland.

7 Young male satin bowerbirds have extraordinary bright blue eyes. Their collages are created using that same blue color almost exclusively. Other varieties of bowerbirds use other colors instead of blue (a bowerbird I saw in San Diego used only kelly green). Some species use many colors at once.

8 When the male birds reach maturity, their eyes become purple. Their eyes expand to a bright, wide stare while they are in the process of attracting the brown-and-green females. Males' feathers turn shiny black with an iridescent rich blue sheen when they get older.

9 After the birds mate, the female leaves the bower. She builds her own nest, lays her eggs, and raises her babies all by herself. The father of the baby birds never participates in the raising of his children.

HOW THEY WORK

1 Bowerbirds create COLLAGES (the word *collage* comes from the French *coller*, "to paste") out of paper, leaves, twigs, fabric, ribbons, beads, bits of wood, pottery, glass, metal, wire, and anything else that they choose, as long as they can carry it. They bring their materials into the space under the bowers they have built, and they begin to create their collages.

2 Their defined working space or "canvas" is the floor space under their bower, which they usually cover with soft green moss for their background.

3 No matter which colors they choose, all varieties of bowerbirds collect and select their pieces because they are visually attracted to them. After they select their pieces, if they decide they no longer like them or if they feel they do not add to their compositions, they reject them.

4 Before making their permanent arrangements, all varieties of bowerbirds move their pieces around until they are completely satisfied with their placement.

5 Bowerbirds sometimes use chewed-up plant matter that adds hints of color when spread onto their bowers.

HOW I WORK

1 My "canvas," always cut to the specific size of my book-to-be, is a piece of heavy white paper. I usually attach another paper (color of my choice) to my heavy under-paper, to become the background.

2 I reject certain scraps just the way a bowerbird does.

3 I keep the particular materials separate for each book while I am working so that I can maintain consistency, page after page.

4 I use tapes and glues to attach the materials to my pages.

5 Although I almost never use any paint, charcoal, pastels, or crayons to add color to my collages, I feel compelled to admit here that sometimes—very, very occasionally—I also might add a hint of a shadow or a blush . . . not never, but really hardly ever.

6 Sometimes when I'm having difficulty figuring out a solution for an image, I get frustrated. Then I can think of fifty reasons to leave my desk—to go for a walk, to bake a cake, to visit a friend, to read the newspaper—and I do leave, at least for a little while.

7 But when I'm really engaged in creating a piece, I seem to forget about everything else: no cooking, no talking, practically no eating, and as the project progresses, I wake up earlier and earlier and I go to sleep later and later.

8 I think I'm driven to those extremes by my curiosity. I just can't wait to see how the finished book will look.

HOW WE ARE THE SAME

1 Bowerbirds and I start out in quite similar ways. We experiment by placing our pieces on our spaces and by moving our pieces around. This is the way we begin to create our compositions.

2 The color, design, and materials of bowerbirds' art are as important to them as they are to me.

3 There is a special aspect of our chosen medium that is appreciated by bowerbirds as well as by me: it is possible to change our minds, and we often do. If, even after working hard to get the collage just right, a second thought tells us that we need to move a shiny paper over just a little, or if we decide that the leaf we stuck on the side detracts instead of adds, a little pulling can always dislodge the piece, and it can be discarded. Another, better piece can always be added later.

4 We, the bowerbirds and I, know that our goals often require many tries, many experiments, and lots of adjustments, but we always try to make the best collages that we can.

5 And, just like bowerbirds, I never know how my collage will look until I finish.

Male Satin Bowerbird
(*Ptilonorhynchus violaceus*)
Queensland, Australia
Copyright: Gary Bell/
OceanwideImages.com

BIBLIOGRAPHY

Attenborough, David. "Story of Life." BBC, 2016.

"The Crazy Courtship of Bowerbirds." BBC, November 20, 2014.

del Hoyo, Joseph, Andrew Elliott, and David A. Christie, eds. *Handbook of the Birds of the World*, Volume 14. Lynx Edicions, 2009.

Gilliard, E. Thomas. *Birds of Paradise and Bower Birds*. AMNH: Natural History Press, 1969.

Frith, Clifford, and Dawn Frith. *Bowerbirds: Nature, Art & History*. Frith & Frith Malanda, 2008.

Frith, Clifford, and Dawn Frith. *The Bowerbirds: Ptilonorhynchidae (Bird Families of the World)*. Oxford University Press, 2004.

Morell, Virginia. "Build It (and they will come)." *National Geographic*, July 2010.

Naiura. *More Tales of My Grandmother's Dreamtime*. Bartel Publications, 2005.

Prum, Richard O. *The Evolution of Beauty: How Darwin's Forgotten Theory of Mate Choice Shapes the Animal World—and Us*. Doubleday, 2017.

Rowland, Peter. *Bowerbirds*. CSIRO Publishing, 2008.

Thank you for your extraordinary help with this project: ornithologists Paul Sweet (American Museum of Natural History), Gerald Borgia (University of Maryland, College Park), Richard Prum (Yale University), Amelia Suarez (San Diego Zoo); my agent, Victoria Wells Arms (Wells Arms Literary); and my personal supporters: JR, AAAH, L and E, NP, JOT, SAC, OG, VWA, DA.